Original title:

Frozen Reflections

Copyright © 2024 Swan Charm

All rights reserved.

Author: Mirell Mesipuu

ISBN HARDBACK: 978-9916-79-975-8

ISBN PAPERBACK: 978-9916-79-976-5

ISBN EBOOK: 978-9916-79-977-2

Delicate Decay in Snowy Embrace

White blankets whisper soft and low,
As time weaves through the falling snow.
Beneath the layers, life decays,
In nature's hand, all slowly fades.

Branches bend with a heavy crown,
Frozen tears on the earth's brown gown.
Yet beauty lingers, subtle, shy,
In the frosted love that bids goodbye.

Traces of a Season in the Stillness

Quiet moments freeze in hues,
Of autumn's breath, the fading views.
Leaves like whispers on the ground,
In the stillness, lost and found.

Ghosts of color linger near,
Echoes of laughter, soft and clear.
As shadows stretch and daylight wanes,
The spirit of change through silence reigns.

Icebound Echoes of the Past

Silent stories wrapped in frost,
Memories linger, but they are lost.
Windows frosted, unclear the view,
History sleeps beneath the blue.

Footsteps traced on glistening white,
Whispers of those who left the light.
Carved in ice, their tales reside,
In frozen chambers, hearts abide.

Shivering Reflections Beneath Starry Skies

Stars adorn the night so bright,
Casting dreams in silver light.
Beneath their watch, the world feels small,
In the quiet, calm, we hear the call.

Cold winds dance through frigid air,
Whispers of wishes, sprinkled fair.
Reflections shiver on the lake,
As morning stirs, and shadows break.

Tides of Silence Beneath the Ice

In the depths where shadows creep,
Echoes whisper, secrets keep.
Frozen waves on crystal seas,
Silent songs in winter's breeze.

Beneath the frost, a world in sleep,
Time stands still, eternity's leap.
Bubbles trapped in icy shells,
Nature's quiet, tranquil spells.

Ghostly figures drift and glide,
In this realm, they softly bide.
Every breath, a tender sigh,
Underneath the cold, grey sky.

The moonlight dances, soft and pale,
Casting dreams on winter's trail.
Secrets linger in the night,
Veiled by shadows, wrapped in light.

Hope is born in frozen dreams,
In the silence, no one screams.
Tides of stillness ebb and flow,
In the depths where cold winds blow.

The Edge of Night in a Frozen World

At the edge where darkness falls,
Snowflakes gather, silence calls.
The stars above, a distant glow,
Whispers of the winds that blow.

Icicles hang like crystalline swords,
Guardians of the ancient woods.
Underneath the pale moon's beam,
Frozen dreams in winter's dream.

Shadows stretch across the white,
Nurturing the depths of night.
Frosted whispers, chilly breath,
Dancing softly, hinting death.

As the twilight starts to fade,
Hidden paths in snow are laid.
A world transformed, so stark, surreal,
In the quiet, secrets conceal.

The edge of night brings tales untold,
In the heart, a warmth to hold.
Frozen kisses, winter's art,
Carving stories on the heart.

Luminescence in the Cold

Soft whispers dance in night,
Stars above, a distant light.
Through the frost, pure magic glows,
In the chill, warm beauty flows.

Silent shadows paint the ground,
In the hush, lost dreams are found.
Breath of winter, crisp and clear,
Echoes of the heart's true cheer.

Frosted branches, silver lace,
Sparkling jewels, nature's grace.
Every flake a world unique,
Beauty in the stillness speaks.

Winds of change weave through the night,
Guiding paths with gentle light.
Moments linger, time stands still,
In this quiet, hearts can fill.

Candle flames against the dark,
Every flicker holds a spark.
In the cold, love's warmth we seek,
In the silence, souls can speak.

Reflections of Solitude in the Snow

Snowflakes fall like whispered thoughts,
Blanketing the world, it's caught.
In the silence, echoes reign,
Filled with peace, yet laced with pain.

Footprints mark a journey rare,
Each a memory left with care.
In the stillness, shadows drift,
Time captures moments, a precious gift.

Frozen scenes in white attire,
Quiet visions, hearts' desire.
Within the solitude we find,
A reflection of the wandering mind.

Beneath the stars, all is bare,
Whispers linger in the air.
In the frost, our stories blend,
In the cold, we seek to mend.

A single tree stands tall and free,
Its branches cradle history.
In solitude, strength can bloom,
As the chill erases gloom.

Frigid Silhouettes of Memory

Shadowed forms in twilight's gleam,
Echoes of a fleeting dream.
In the cold, past whispers soar,
Memories knock at winter's door.

Each frost-kissed leaf whispers past,
Stories etched that forever last.
In frozen nights, we tread with care,
Trace the lines of love laid bare.

Figures dance in ghostly light,
Remnants linger through the night.
Time's embrace, both soft and strong,
In the cold, we find belong.

Silent echoes of laughter fade,
In the frost, our paths are laid.
Footsteps lost but never gone,
In frigid air, our hearts move on.

Through the chill, a warmth we greet,
Past and present softly meet.
Frigid silhouettes tell the tale,
Of love's journey, undeterred, we sail.

The Art of Stillness in Time

In quiet moments, hearts find rest,
The art of stillness, nature's best.
Time unfolds like petals rare,
In the calm, we breathe in air.

Fleeting days drift slowly by,
In stillness, we let out a sigh.
Each second, a delicate thread,
Woven through what lies ahead.

Snowflakes cradle gentle peace,
In their fall, our worries cease.
Stillness whispers, softly calls,
Within its touch, the chaos falls.

Beneath the stars, we linger here,
In the night, all becomes clear.
The art of being, pure and true,
In quietude, we find the view.

Moments stretch like shadows long,
Wrapped in silence, we belong.
In the heart of winter's sigh,
The art of stillness teaches why.

Still Epiphanies of Winter's Chill

Silent whispers in the night,
Dreams descend in soft moonlight.
Frosty breath of twilight's grace,
Time stands still, a warm embrace.

Gentle snowflakes, pure and bright,
Lending magic to the night.
Each still moment, softly gleams,
Cradled deep within our dreams.

Ethereal shadows dance and sway,
Nature's heart begins to play.
Beneath the stars, a tranquil scene,
Awakens wonders unforeseen.

Fingers tracing on a pane,
Memories linger, sweet refrain.
In the chill, our spirits sigh,
Connected to the endless sky.

Stillness holds us, here we dwell,
In the winter's sacred shell.
Each epiphany we find,
Unlocks treasures of the mind.

Elysian Fields under a Frosted Sky

Veils of white across the land,
Nature whispers, soft and grand.
Underneath a frosted hue,
Dreams unfold in shades anew.

Crystalline branches reach for light,
Fragrant air, a pure delight.
Footsteps mark the softest ground,
Quiet moments, peace profound.

Twilight casts a glowing grace,
Time slows down in this embrace.
Elysium, where souls reside,
Awaits the warmth we often hide.

In the distance, echoes call,
Winter scatters, leaves a thrall.
With each breath, the stillness grows,
In this realm, the spirit flows.

Together lost in twilight's pull,
Hearts awaken, vessels full.
Frosted skies, a blanket wide,
Cradle dreams that never hide.

Solitude in a Sea of White

A quiet hush envelops all,
Amidst the snow, I hear its call.
In solitude, I find my peace,
Winter's chill brings sweet release.

Blankets soft, a timeless shroud,
Wisdom wrapped in silence loud.
Footprints vanish, none remain,
Nature's cloak holds every gain.

Glimmers sparkle in the sun,
A world transformed, a race not run.
In this realm, the heart does see,
Solitude sets the spirit free.

Branches bow with heavy grace,
In the still, a warm embrace.
Moments linger, soft and light,
In this sea of endless white.

Harbor dreams within the chill,
Let the silence be your will.
Alone yet not, the heart will know,
In solitude, the spirit grows.

Crystal Clear in the Distance

A glimmer shines beyond the haze,
Crystal clear in winter's maze.
Truth unveiled in frosty breath,
Life awakens, overcoming death.

Mountains rise, a distant dream,
Silhouettes in twilight's gleam.
Every whisper holds a spark,
Illuminating the stark.

Windswept whispers call my name,
In their echo, life's a game.
Pathway winding, shadows blend,
Where the clear horizons bend.

Frozen lakes mirror the sky,
Reflecting hopes that never die.
In the distance, visions rear,
Crystal clear, I hold them dear.

As sunset paints the world in gold,
New stories waiting to unfold.
Every heartbeat's a dance so bright,
In the distance, I find my light.

The Glassy Surface of Forgotten Moments

Reflections on the water,
A quiet, still façade.
Whispers of the past echo,
In the shimmer of the pond.

Each ripple tells a story,
Of laughter, love, and tears.
Time suspended in a moment,
Mirroring our hidden fears.

A fragile veil of silence,
Covers secrets long concealed.
Beneath this glassy surface,
Lives the heart that once revealed.

In twilight's gentle grasp,
Memories seem to fade.
Yet in the stillness lingers,
The warmth of joys once made.

We walk along the margins,
Tracing paths we used to roam.
In the glassy hue of twilight,
We find the way back home.

Beneath the Surface

The depths hold quiet secrets,
Beneath the waves they lie.
Tides of time wash over them,
While the surface days go by.

A world that breathes in shadows,
And dances in the dark.
With whispers of an ocean's song,
Where silence leaves its mark.

The stories of each current,
Weaving tales of lost and found.
In depths of blue and mystery,
Life's wonders are unbound.

We plunge into the unknown,
Seeking treasures lost to time.
In the cool embrace of water,
We learn the art of rhyme.

Beneath the surface, magic dwells,
In every ebb and flow.
For in the heart of darkness,
Is where the true light glows.

History Lies

In pages worn and tattered,
We find the truth entwined.
Yet history can be a mirror,
Reflecting what's maligned.

Stories crafted nicely,
By those who wield the pen.
But beneath the polished surface,
Lurk shadows of the men.

Each era spins its fables,
A tapestry of dreams.
Some truths are left unspoken,
As time unravels seams.

We dance around the whispers,
Of legends told with pride.
But in the heart of knowing,
Lies what it tries to hide.

History can cloak its secrets,
In layers soft and thick.
To find the hidden stories,
We must be brave and quick.

Icicle Dreams at Dusk

Dripping silver from the eaves,
Icicles hang in grace.
Whispers of the evening chill,
Glisten in a quiet space.

Each shard a frozen longing,
Captured in the twilight glow.
Dreams of warmth and summer days,
In a world wrapped in snow.

The sky bleeds shades of orange,
As day slips into night.
Beneath the weight of winter,
Icicles hold their light.

In the hush of falling dusk,
The world holds its breath tight.
Each icicle, a promise,
Of dawn breaking the night.

We chase the fleeting moments,
With hearts both bold and meek.
For in those icicles' beauty,
Lie dreams we dare to seek.

Frosted Memories Unraveled

Crystals dance on window panes,
Like stories from the past.
Frosted memories unfold,
In whispers that can't last.

Each breath a fleeting echo,
A ghost of warmth inside.
In the chill of winter's grasp,
Our tender thoughts reside.

Unraveling the moments,
With every glistening flake.
In the frost lies the promise,
Of warmth the heart will make.

We weave through frozen pathways,
With laughter and with tears.
Each frosted memory cherished,
Through the passage of our years.

In the beauty of the frost,
We find the love we seek.
For even in the coldest,
Our hearts will never leak.

Still Waters on a Frosted Lens

Quiet ripples stir the night,
Beneath a sky with twinkling light.
Reflections dance, a soft embrace,
In stillness found, a sacred space.

Frosted edges kiss the rim,
Nature's touch, both wild and dim.
Echoes whisper through the trees,
As silence drapes upon the breeze.

Shadows play in moonlit glow,
Each heartbeat's pulse, so soft and slow.
The world feels hushed, a breathless hush,
Nature's beauty, in this rush.

Ripples blend with starry skies,
A canvas bright where truth lies.
In every gaze, a glimpse of peace,
A moment's pause, a sweet release.

Still waters hold a timeless song,
In their depths, we all belong.
Through frosted lens, our spirits soar,
In quiet nights, we search for more.

Mirror Heartbeats in the Snow

Footprints whisper on the path,
In frosty air, we share a laugh.
With every step, our hearts align,
In this white world, our souls entwine.

Silver flakes fall, soft and slow,
Each one a secret, a gentle glow.
We trace the lines of warmth and cold,
In winter's arms, we are consoled.

Glances shared amidst the shade,
Reflections dance, love is made.
Underneath the pale moonlight,
Our mirror heartbeats feel just right.

Branches cradle snow with grace,
In this still world, we find our place.
With hands held tight, we carve our fate,
In mirrored joy, we celebrate.

The night deepens, stars awake,
A constellation in our wake.
With heartbeats matched in snowy bliss,
In every breath, we find our kiss.

Winter's Silhouette in Stillness

The trees stand tall, a silent watch,
In winter's grip, we feel the swatch.
Shadows stretch beneath the moon,
In twilight's hush, our hearts attune.

Silhouettes against the night,
Embrace the chill, find pure delight.
With every rustle, whispers sigh,
Beneath the stars, the world drifts by.

Softly wrap in cozy wraps,
As frost unfolds its lacing traps.
Each breath a cloud, we drift and sway,
In winter's arms, we wish to stay.

A quiet peace fills every space,
In stillness found, the softest grace.
With every heartbeat, time stands still,
In winter's hush, we find our will.

Glistening dreams in frozen air,
Moments cherished, pure and rare.
As winter's silhouette glows bright,
We dance together through the night.

Iced Thoughts in Dim Light

In shadows cast by candle's glow,
Iced thoughts drift soft, like falling snow.
A mind awash in mellow hue,
Illuminated by the truth.

The flickering flame tells tales untold,
Of whispered hopes and dreams of old.
In dim light's warmth, we share our fears,
A symphony that calms our tears.

Frozen moments, memories freeze,
Captured echoes in winter's breeze.
With every sigh, the world unwinds,
In fragile peace, serenity finds.

The night envelopes, a velvet shroud,
With honesty that speaks so loud.
In the quiet, our souls ignite,
Iced thoughts warm in the dim light.

Each flicker a promise, a story spun,
In the heart's embrace, two become one.
As the world outside feels cold and stark,
In dim light, together, we spark.

Icicles of Memory

Hanging from the eaves, so bright,
They catch the sun and shimmer light.
Each drip a tale of days gone by,
Frozen whispers in the sky.

In winter's grasp, they bend and sway,
A fragile dance, a cold ballet.
They hold the past in crystal form,
An artful echo from the storm.

Like dreams that linger, soft and clear,
These shards of time bring distant cheer.
Each glint a spark, a fleeting spark,
Of moments spent in winter's dark.

As seasons turn, they'll fade away,
Yet in the heart, they ever stay.
A frozen tribute, sweet and rare,
To memories that linger there.

In twilight's glow, they softly gleam,
A tapestry of hope and dream.
Icicles hang, a silent sigh,
Holding stories in the sky.

Shattered Glass Beneath the Ice

Underneath the frozen sheen,
Lies a world once bright and green.
Cracked reflections, light displays,
Haunting echoes of lost days.

With each step, a sound that breaks,
Fractured whispers, silence shakes.
Memories trapped in crystal clear,
Awakened by the winter's sneer.

Beyond the glass, the shadows creep,
Secrets buried, dark and deep.
A story told in shards and dust,
The icy grip, a frozen rust.

Yet hope survives, though edges fray,
In each splinter, a glimmered ray.
Life underneath begins to stir,
Awakening in dreams that were.

Shattered glass, a canvas bright,
Reflecting shadows, bathing light.
Beneath the ice, the heart beats strong,
In the silence, we belong.

Echoes in the Snow

Whispers float on frosty air,
Echoes linger everywhere.
Footsteps soft on winter's sheet,
Silent stories, bittersweet.

Each flake that falls, a tale retold,
In patterns brave, both new and old.
They dance around in quiet grace,
Softening the world's harsh face.

Underneath the moon's soft glow,
Time stands still, yet continues flow.
Every breath is a misty plume,
Drawing warmth in winter's gloom.

Voices fade but never cease,
In the stillness, find your peace.
Nature's hymn, a soothing sound,
In the drifts, our dreams are found.

Echoes in the snow remain,
Holding joy, embracing pain.
In the chill, the heart beats warm,
Finding solace in the storm.

Crystal Dreams on Slumbering Lakes

Beneath the ice, the water sleeps,
Where mirrored worlds in silence keep.
Dreams encased in winter's might,
A glimmering, tranquil sight.

Whispers ripple beneath the chill,
Secrets waiting, time to fill.
Crystal visions softly call,
In the stillness, we find it all.

The surface glows with lunar hue,
As stars above bid night adieu.
In this realm where dreams are spun,
Every heartbeat's just begun.

Frosted edges fragility show,
Yet life pulsates, as rivers flow.
Through the glass, visions merge and blend,
Creating stories without end.

Crystal dreams, serene embrace,
In slumbering lakes, we find our place.
A world of peace beneath the skies,
Where every soul in stillness lies.

Shimmering Silence of the Season

In the hush of falling snow,
Whispers of winter softly glow.
A blanket white on slumbering earth,
Cradling dreams, giving birth.

Twinkling stars in a midnight sky,
While gentle breezes softly sigh.
Trees stand tall, a silver hue,
Wrapped in silence, pure and true.

Footsteps fade on the crisp white ground,
In this tranquil space, peace is found.
Each flake that dances from the night,
A fleeting moment of pure delight.

The world pauses, holds its breath,
In shimmering silence, a gentle death.
Nature speaks in quiet tones,
As beauty reigns in frozen zones.

From dusk till dawn, the chill persists,
With frosted air that softly twists.
Season's end will soon be here,
But in this silence, we persevere.

Landscapes of the Heart in Winter Light

In winter's grip, the world transforms,
A canvas blank, where stillness warms.
Muted tones of grey and white,
Craft landscapes bathed in quiet light.

Beneath the frost, a pulse remains,
In barren branches, truth retains.
Hearts entwined in whispered snow,
Where memories linger, ebb, and flow.

The sun dips low, a golden sheen,
Illuminating all that's been.
Fractured dreams like icicles hang,
In soulful echoes, the heart will sang.

Through frosty fields, our shadows stretch,
In every step, our souls connect.
A landscape rich with tales untold,
In winter's chill, we find the bold.

With every breath, the cold ignites,
A fire within, that warms the nights.
In the quietude, we learn to see,
The heart's landscapes, wild and free.

Icebound Stories of Old

In the stillness of the frigid air,
Whispers echo from everywhere.
Tales of ages locked in ice,
Treasured secrets that entice.

Old trees stand with stories grand,
Witness to the shifting land.
Branches heavy, tales unfold,
In frozen moments, heroes bold.

Rivers pause beneath a shroud,
Nature's breath held, quiet, loud.
Silent songs of seasons gone,
In crystal prisons, dreams live on.

Footprints marked in snow so deep,
Carving paths that memories keep.
Echoes linger in the night,
Icebound stories, entwined in light.

As dawn breaks through the biting chill,
Legends rise, and hearts must fill.
With every thaw, a tale reborn,
In the warmth of the coming dawn.

The Weight of White on the Soul

A heavy cloak, the world transformed,
In purity, the vision's warmed.
Beneath the weight of endless snow,
Ancient whispers start to flow.

Each flake a story waiting to tell,
In the silence, we are compelled.
To pause, to feel, beneath the weight,
Soulful moments that resonate.

The burden lifts with every breath,
In this stillness, life finds depth.
Frosty breath dances in the light,
A fragile beauty, soul's delight.

Through the drifts, the heart beats slow,
As nature's pulse begins to flow.
A reminder in white, profound,
That stillness often speaks its sound.

When spring arrives and takes its hold,
The weight will shift, but stories told.
Remaining echoes in our core,
The weight of white forevermore.

Silent Whispers of Winter

Soft snowflakes drift down,
A blanket for the earth.
Whispers of frost in the air,
Nature pauses in mirth.

Bare branches stand tall,
Cradling dreams of the spring.
The world wrapped in silence,
Winter's gentle offering.

Footsteps echo softly,
In a world draped in white.
Each crunch tells a story,
Of shadows in the light.

Stars pierce the dark sky,
Like diamonds above the cold.
The night breathes a promise,
Of warmth yet to unfold.

In this tranquil moment,
Time hangs by a thread.
Silent whispers surround,
Where the heart dares to tread.

Fractured Light in Hibernation

Shadows dance on the wall,
As the sun begins to fade.
Light fractures in the still,
Painting dusk with a blade.

A flicker in the twilight,
Hope glimmers then slips by.
In the silence of the night,
Stars weave stories on high.

Winter's breath is heavy,
Cloaked in a shimmering mist.
Hidden dreams lie dormant,
In a world wrapped and kissed.

Every corner holds echoes,
Of warmth in past embrace.
Light's delicate reminder,
In this quiet space.

Hibernation whispers,
Of life waiting to rise.
Fractured light will return,
To paint over the skies.

Glacial Traces of Yesterday

Frozen rivers tell tales,
Of movements long ago.
Each glacier bears witness,
To the ebb and the flow.

Ancient whispers ripple,
In the heart of the ice.
Time carved its path slowly,
With precision and grace.

Beneath layers of silence,
Memories long preserved.
Traces of what once was,
In the frost, they swerved.

The weight of the stillness,
Hangs heavy in the air.
Glacial forms remind us,
Of journeys that we share.

As the sun kisses softly,
The cold begins to yield.
Glacial traces shimmer,
In the warmth revealed.

The Stillness between Breaths

Eyes closed to the world,
A moment held in time.
In the stillness we linger,
Finding peace in the rhyme.

The pause before the heartbeat,
A breath drawn deep and slow.
In this fragile silence,
We unravel what we know.

Thoughts drift like the clouds,
In an endless blue sea.
The space that holds us gently,
Where we're meant to be.

Each heartbeat a reminder,
Of life's delicate dance.
In the stillness between breaths,
We find our sacred chance.

Embrace the quiet moments,
Let the noise fade away.
In stillness, we are anchored,
In the light of the day.

Still Waters Running Deep in the Cold

In silent pools the ice does form,
A mirror of the quiet storm.
Beneath the surface, secrets hide,
As winter's breath flows, deep and wide.

The trees stand tall with branches bare,
Their shadows dance in frosty air.
Whispers of the past take flight,
In the stillness of the night.

Crystals glisten, nature's art,
A frozen canvas, nature's heart.
Ripples weave through frozen dreams,
As nature sighs and softly gleams.

Still waters hold a story deep,
Where time freezes and secrets sleep.
In every nook, in every seam,
Awaits the magic of the dream.

Here in the cold, we find our peace,
A moment's pause, a sweet release.
With each reflection, life does flow,
In stillness, beauty starts to grow.

Reflections of Light in Subzero Glow

In the twilight, frost begins to gleam,
Each crystal holds a flickering dream.
A tapestry of stars unfolds,
In silver threads, the night beholds.

The moonlight dances on icy streams,
Awakening the heart with silent themes.
A canvas bright, with glimmers bold,
Whispers of warmth in the bitter cold.

From frosty breath, new worlds arise,
As light plays tricks beneath the skies.
In shadows deep, reflections wait,
To show us paths we dare to take.

Illuminated dreams, unconfined,
In every flake, a truth we find.
They twinkle softly, a soothing call,
In the depths of winter's sprawling hall.

Let the glow guide our wandering hearts,
Through chilly nights and frozen arts.
In subzero warmth, we weave our tales,
As light and shadows dance in gales.

Hushed Conversations with Winter's Spirit

In the hush of winter's breath,
Whispers linger, life and death.
A spirit stirs in shadows deep,
Where silent secrets softly creep.

Through winding paths of frosted air,
We pause to listen, souls laid bare.
With gentle sighs, the trees concede,
To winter's warm, embracing need.

In quiet moments, frost does speak,
A language found in icy streaks.
Invisible threads of life intertwine,
In hushed confessions, so divine.

The world slows down to hear the call,
Of winter's spirit, embracing all.
In every flake, a story spun,
Of battles fought and victories won.

So let us wander, hearts aglow,
In hushed conversations, let thoughts flow.
Through winter's grasp, we find our peace,
In frozen moments, sweet release.

Mosaic of Frost on Branches

A tapestry of ice unfolds,
Upon the branches, beauty holds.
Each tiny shard a story told,
In the embrace of winter's cold.

The boughs adorned, a work of art,
Nature's touch, a frozen heart.
With every breath, the magic glows,
In every crystal, life bestows.

Patterns weave and sparkle bright,
Creating wonders in pale light.
As nature paints in shades of white,
A mosaic born of frosty night.

From dusk till dawn, the scene transforms,
In winter's arms, serenity warms.
Among the branches, echoes play,
In a winter's dance, come what may.

Through whispered winds, the stories flow,
A memory in frozen show.
A world adorned, so pure, so deep,
In winter's cradle, dreams do sleep.

Mirror Images in the Frost

In the morning light, they gleam,
Frozen whispers of a dream.
Patterns crisp, reflections bright,
Nature's art in silvered light.

Each breath visible, a ghostly sigh,
Trees adorned, they wave goodbye.
Branches etched in icy lace,
Time stands still, a frozen grace.

Quiet echoes in the air,
Each layer speaks of tender care.
World transformed in this embrace,
A moment held in nature's space.

A Glimpse Through the Snowfall

Gentle flakes begin to fall,
Whispers soft, a silent call.
Covering ground with silver white,
A wonderland, pure delight.

Footprints hidden, paths erased,
Memories in snowflakes placed.
Laughter shared beneath the pines,
Joy cascades like winter vines.

Branches bow with added weight,
Frosted dreams that captivate.
A glimpse of peace in every flake,
A canvas fresh, the world awake.

Chilled Shadows of Time

As the sun dips low and fades,
Shadows stretch, in twilight's shades.
Cold encroaches, night draws near,
Whispers linger, crystal clear.

Memories cast in shades of gray,
Time stands still, the night at play.
Frosty breath upon the ground,
Chilled secrets lost, yet found.

Softly now, the quiet deep,
Through the shadows, silence creeps.
In this stillness, hearts rewind,
Reflections of a past defined.

Ethereal Patterns on a Frozen Canvas

A vast expanse, a canvas pure,
Each frost-kissed trace, a delicate cure.
Intricate lace in nature's hand,
Beauty blooms in this frostbit land.

Sunrise dances on icy beams,
Awakening winter's tender dreams.
Each pattern tells a tale of old,
Ethereal whispers, secrets told.

Colors shift as shadows play,
On the canvas, night and day.
A fleeting art, a moment caught,
In frost's embrace, we find what's sought.

Delicate Suspense of the Deep

In shadows deep, the silence stirs,
A soft caress, where nothing blurs.
Waves whisper tales, secrets to share,
Moonlight glints, weaving dreams in the air.

In depths untold, a world profound,
Mysteries beckon, lost yet found.
A subtle pull, the tide's embrace,
In this stillness, time finds its place.

Echoes linger, the ocean sighs,
Wonders drift beneath the skies.
Each ripple holds a story dear,
In the tranquil deep, we draw near.

A fragile thread binds heart to sea,
In tender moments, we are free.
Suspense unfolds with each soft wave,
In the depths, our souls we save.

An endless dance, a lover's leap,
In delicate suspense, the secrets keep.
A breath held tight in the watery gloom,
A promise whispers from the moon's bloom.

Shimmering Memories Entombed

In dusty corners, stories hide,
Shimmering echoes, time's sweet guide.
Fragments glint with a golden hue,
Memories linger, both old and new.

Through faded frames, the past will speak,
Whispers of love, a gentle peak.
Each glance reveals a time once bright,
In shadows cast, dreams take flight.

Forgotten halls, where laughter played,
Softened light through curtains swayed.
Eternal moments, forever sealed,
In heart's embrace, pain is healed.

In time's embrace, the shimmer glows,
A tapestry of highs and lows.
We journey forth, yet pause to see,
Shimmering memories, a part of me.

Entombed in love's eternal hold,
In whispered tales, life's truth is told.
A dance of past, in present's grace,
Memories shimmer, time can't erase.

Cold Glimmers of the Heart

In twilight's hush, a chill descends,
Cold glimmers stir where silence bends.
A fragile beat, a distant song,
Heart's quiet rhythm where dreams belong.

Beneath the frost, a warmth resides,
Hidden deep, where hope abides.
In quiet moments, the pulse reveals,
Silent whispers that love conceals.

Each glimmer bright, a spark of light,
Through darkest nights, it shines so bright.
Though icy winds may bite and tear,
The heart endures, still tender care.

Broken pieces weave a tale,
In coldest depths, we shall not pale.
For every glimmer that fades away,
A brighter dawn waits, come what may.

In every chill, warmth finds its pride,
Glimmers of heart, no need to hide.
In courage found through trials stark,
Love reigns true, igniting the dark.

Ethereal Echoes in the Breeze

In the soft sigh of the evening breeze,
Whispers of life dance through the trees.
Ethereal echoes call from afar,
Guiding our dreams like a wandering star.

With every rustle, a haunting tune,
Carried softly by the silver moon.
Fleeting shadows weave through the night,
Gentle reminders of lost light.

In quietude, the world takes pause,
In the whispers, we find our cause.
Echoes of laughter, of joy and pain,
In the breeze we feel life's refrain.

Each fluttering leaf holds a memory dear,
In the subtle hush, the heart draws near.
A symphony played on nature's stage,
Ethereal echoes, an ancient page.

With every gust, a story unfolds,
In wind's embrace, our spirit beholds.
From dusk to dawn, in harmony's weave,
Echoes in the breeze, we choose to believe.

Shards of Beauty in the Freeze

In the quiet, crystals glint,
Every breath, a muffled hint.
Fragments dance with frozen grace,
Time surrenders, a soft embrace.

Nature rests in diamond's glow,
Whispers linger, winds that blow.
Shattered light upon the ground,
Silent stories to be found.

Snowflakes twirl in fragile art,
Each a piece, a beating heart.
Glistening on branches bare,
Moments frozen, caught in air.

A canvas white, so pure and bright,
Underneath, the world ignites.
Beauty lies in each sharp break,
A tranquil pause, the stillness makes.

As day fades to twilight hue,
Shards like stars in evening blue.
In the freeze, a truth revealed,
In the silence, joy concealed.

Chilling Mists of Reflection

Veils of gray upon the lake,
Softest whispers, memories wake.
In the fog, thoughts intertwine,
Chilling mists, like aged wine.

Mirrored stones, deep secrets hold,
Stories told in hues of cold.
Breathless echoes through the night,
Ghostly forms take gentle flight.

Fallen leaves weave paths untold,
Nature's tapestry, bold yet cold.
Each reflection, fragments past,
In this silence, shadows cast.

Frosted edges on the trees,
Carried softly on the breeze.
Chilling moments, fleeting trust,
In the mist, we turn to dust.

Rippling water, still yet deep,
In its embrace, the world will sleep.
Chilling mists, where thoughts collide,
In reflections, fears abide.

Twilight's Embrace on the Ice

The world glazed in twilight's hue,
Softly kissed by night's debut.
Shadows stretch across the land,
Whispers call, delicate and planned.

Icicles drip with frozen sighs,
Beneath the vast and starry skies.
As darkness falls, colors blend,
Nature's palette starts to mend.

On the ice, a dance unfolds,
Stories simple, yet so bold.
Moonlight glimmers, secrets shared,
In this moment, hearts are bared.

Breath of winter, cool, serene,
In twilight's embrace, we glean.
Time slows down, an endless night,
Lost in dreams, harboring light.

Cold caress, an aching peace,
In the stillness, we find release.
Twilight whispers softly near,
In its embrace, we shed our fear.

Nature's Palate of Winter

Vivid strokes of white and gray,
Nature's art in stark display.
Splashes bright on canvas bare,
Winter's brush, beyond compare.

Crisp air hangs with life anew,
Beneath the snow, a hidden view.
Every flake a tale to weave,
In this palette, we believe.

Branches painted, frost-kissed tips,
Nature's poetry in silent scripts.
Colors muted, yet so bold,
In each hue, stories unfold.

Underneath a quilt of dreams,
Quiet magic softly seems.
Winter's whispers, soft and slow,
In this beauty, love will grow.

A palette rich, yet pure and true,
Hearts awaken, bright with dew.
In every breath, a masterpiece,
Nature's gift, our souls released.

Fractured Light on Snow

Gentle sunbeams break the dawn,
Casting shadows long and drawn.
Snowflakes dance in a quiet breeze,
Whispers of winter's soft unease.

Crystals glitter, pure and bright,
Nature's canvas, a stunning sight.
Each step crunched beneath my feet,
Echoes of silence, bitter sweet.

Beneath the surface, stories lie,
Frozen moments that swiftly fly.
Fractured light on snowflakes reign,
Memories linger, joy and pain.

The world holds its breath, peaceful sway,
As twilight drapes the end of day.
Colors blend, the sky's embrace,
A fleeting glimpse of time and space.

Stars twinkle down in tranquil night,
Bathing everything in silver light.
Embracing dreams that softly flow,
In the beauty of fractured snow.

Silence in a Silver Veil

Mist envelops the lonely wood,
A hush that whispers, understood.
Nature cloaked in moonlit grace,
Silence lingers in this space.

Shadows flicker like candle flames,
Playing shy, forgetting names.
Veils of silver, soft and still,
Night embraces, brings its thrill.

Footsteps muffled, secrets kept,
In the silence, dreams are swept.
Each breath held in the frosted air,
Untold stories drift with care.

Branches weave a soothing song,
Echoing the dusk so long.
A tapestry of whispered thoughts,
In this silence, wisdom's caught.

Time stands still, wrapped in the night,
Lost in shadows, out of sight.
Under stars, in silver's embrace,
Silence weaves its timeless lace.

Icy Portraits of Yesterday

Captured moments, cold and bright,
Icy portraits of yesterday's light.
Faces frozen in fleeting time,
Memories linger, soft as rhyme.

Frosted whispers in the air,
Silent echoes everywhere.
Windows to the past we seek,
In icy canvases, voices speak.

Sunrise paints a muted glow,
Shadows dance on fallen snow.
Each imprint tells a tale of old,
Of laughter shared and hearts of gold.

Time reflects in every flake,
Worn textures, a tender ache.
In the stillness, we find our way,
Guided by the past's display.

Through frosted glass, we glimpse anew,
The art of life, in vibrant hue.
Icy portraits of what has been,
Capture echoes of the unseen.

Frosted Facets of Time

Glistening patterns in morning light,
Frosted facets, a beautiful sight.
Each shard reflects a story told,
Moments captured, both young and old.

The wind carries whispers of days,
Dancing lightly in playful ways.
Memories glimmer as time unfolds,
In the warmth of the sun, they hold.

Every glimmer reveals the past,
Echoes of laughter meant to last.
Time's embrace, a kindred dance,
In the snow's blanket, hearts enhance.

With every freeze, a reminder near,
Of journeys taken, paths so clear.
Frosted facets, a prism bright,
Displaying dreams in soft twilight.

Beneath the surface, time does play,
Crafting the moments, come what may.
Frosted facets, treasures found,
In the silence, love is unbound.

Ice Petals in a Winter Garden

In the hush of the frost-kissed night,
Delicate whispers take flight.
Each petal a crystal, pure and bright,
Dancing softly in soft moonlight.

Branches adorned with a silvery lace,
Nature's artistry, a stunning embrace.
Silent beauty in this frozen space,
Held in time, a tranquil place.

Snowflakes twirl in a gentle spin,
Filling the garden, a soft, white skin.
Underneath lies the warmth within,
Awaiting spring where life begins.

Breath of winter, cold and clear,
Each moment cherished, held so dear.
Whispers of spring seem drawing near,
Promising blooms that will soon appear.

In this winter garden, dreams align,
Ice petals glowing, a soft design.
A fleeting moment, pure and divine,
Nature's splendor, a quiet sign.

Wrap of Cold Over Dreams Deferred

Wrapped in blankets of frost and chill,
Dreams are frozen, wandering still.
Whispers echo of hopes to fulfill,
While time marches on, against its will.

In the stillness, a quiet sigh,
The warmth of longing asks us why.
Underneath a gray, heavy sky,
A spark still lingers, though it's shy.

Shadows stretch long in the pale light,
As the day dims into the night.
Memories dance just out of sight,
Wrapped in cold, they hold on tight.

Silent wishes rest beneath the ice,
Fragile fantasies, a game of dice.
Promises linger, but they think twice,
In the wrap of cold, we pay a price.

Yet within this frozen, patient heart,
Beneath the layers, dreams still start.
For spring will come, a brand new art,
To thaw the fears, and play its part.

Luminous Echoes in the Icebound Dawn

Morning breaks on a crystal sea,
Luminous echoes call to me.
In the stillness, I feel so free,
Nature's beauty, pure decree.

Icebound branches glisten and shine,
Caught in a moment, divine design.
Each flake, a star, in its own line,
Tales of wonder, ancient, intertwine.

Whispers of dawn kiss the cold air,
A symphony soft, beyond compare.
Painting the world with hues so rare,
Lifting the heart from dark despair.

In this frozen landscape, dreams awake,
Tracing the edges, I start to take.
Each breath a promise, a gentle quake,
Awakening hope for the future's sake.

With every heartbeat, shadows recede,
Luminous echoes plant the seed.
In the icebound dawn, we're all freed,
To harvest the dreams that we all need.

A Shard of Time Encased in Snow

A shard of time lies buried deep,
Encased in snow where shadows creep.
Memories frozen, secrets to keep,
Slumbering softly, lost in sleep.

With every gust, the whispers show,
Stories hidden beneath the snow.
In the stillness, a tale will grow,
Of moments cherished, long ago.

Footprints fade on the wintry lane,
Echoes linger of joy and pain.
Each flake that falls, a soft refrain,
Marking time in this cold domain.

Underneath the winter's shroud,
Life still pulses, though hidden and proud.
Waiting for light to break the cloud,
Dreams lay still, but life is allowed.

So we honor this quiet grace,
A shard of time, a frozen space.
In the heart of winter's embrace,
Hope will bloom and time will pace.

The Art of Winter's Remembrance

Snowflakes fall like whispered dreams,
Covering earth in silver seams.
Silent nights, the stars align,
Frosted breath, a moment divine.

Echoes of warmth in colder air,
Memories linger, soft and rare.
In the stillness, shadows play,
Winter's art, both night and day.

Trees stand bare with graceful pride,
In their silence, secrets hide.
Each branch tells tales of yore,
Seasons passed, forevermore.

Underneath the frozen sky,
Time unfurls, but moments fly.
Each heartbeat etched in crystal glow,
In winter's grasp, we come to know.

Radiance Beneath the Ice

Beneath the chill, a warmth awaits,
Hidden treasures as time skates.
Diamonds dance on frosty beams,
Whispers trapped in icy dreams.

Shimmers break the surface still,
Nature's pCanvas, a tranquil thrill.
In the glistening, hopes ignite,
Resilience cloaked in winter's bite.

Waves of blue in depths below,
Secrets hibernate, yet glow.
Echoes of life in frozen streams,
Silent witnesses to ancient dreams.

Fragments of light in muted hues,
A symphony of winter's blues.
Beneath the ice, the world holds tight,
Radiance sleeps, awaiting light.

Ephemeral Glimmer in the Mists

In the mists of morning light,
Glimmers fade, an ethereal sight.
Fog embraces the waking ground,
Whispers of dreams, no longer found.

Softly woven, the air feels thick,
Time drips slowly, like a flick.
A moment held, then slipped away,
Like shadows dancing in the gray.

Delicate threads of silver lace,
Emerge from winter's cold embrace.
Each breath a cloud, ephemeral sighs,
Mirrors of life in transient skies.

Fleeting visions fade with the dawn,
Nature's tapestry gently drawn.
In the silence, beauty sings,
Ephemeral gifts that winter brings.

Celestial Reflections on Chilled Surfaces

Stars mirror on a frozen lake,
Heavens whisper, as stillness takes.
Each glimmer captured, a fleeting kiss,
In icy realms, we find our bliss.

Night unfolds, the world in black,
Celestial wonders lighting the track.
Ripples dance, a cosmic play,
The universe holds us, night and day.

Beneath the frost, a pulse remains,
Every shimmer tells of chains.
In the quiet, hope reflects,
Chilled surfaces hold our connects.

As we gaze into the abyss,
Finding solace in moments missed.
Celestial dreams in winter's sweep,
In silent nights, our spirits leap.

Tranquil Visions in the Cold Light

In shadows cast by silver glow,
Where whispers dance and breezes flow,
A world adorned in icy grace,
Embraced by time's soft, tender trace.

Beneath the stars, the silence hums,
As frosty winds through stillness comes,
Each breath a cloud, so faint, so brief,
In frozen dreams, we find relief.

From glistening branches, crystals weep,
In tranquil night, the secrets keep,
A canvas white with hopes anew,
In cold light's reach, the heart breaks through.

The moon hangs low, a sentinel bright,
Guiding lost souls through the night,
While echoes of a distant song,
Remind us where we once belonged.

In this ethereal, frozen space,
We touch the warmth of soft embrace,
And hold the visions with delight,
In tranquil moments, pure and bright.

The Waiting Heart Beneath the Ice

A heart encased in frosty dreams,
Beneath the surface, silence screams,
In winter's grasp, it beats alone,
A fragile pulse, a whispered tone.

Each flake of snow, a tale untold,
Of warmth concealed, of love so bold,
Yet wrapped in layers, cold and tight,
The waiting heart yearns for the light.

A glimmer shines through icy seams,
Awakening forgotten dreams,
With every thaw, a spark ignites,
In tender warmth, the heart unites.

Beneath this shroud of crystal white,
The embers glow, a hopeful sight,
For in the depths, desire sleeps,
Awaiting spring, its promise keeps.

The waiting heart shall find its voice,
In seasons' change, it will rejoice,
As ice will melt and shadows flee,
To dance again, to be set free.

Whispers of a Thawing Past

In gentle breezes, whispers rise,
Of yesterdays beneath the skies,
As ice retreats, the echoes play,
Bringing warmth to light the way.

Forgotten tales in softest sighs,
Awoken now, like fragile flies,
They flutter forth on warming air,
To weave the memories we share.

Each droplet falls, a note in song,
Of loves we knew, of where we belong,
The past slips free, like melting snow,
In every heart, a seed to grow.

As shadows yield to golden rays,
The remnants of those colder days,
Fade gently into the embrace,
Of present moments, full of grace.

Whispers linger, soft and sweet,
In thawing depths, where summers meet,
With every dawn, the world renews,
As life returns, and love ensues.

Alabaster Fables in the Winter Light

In winter's realm of alabaster,
Where stories breathe and echoes master,
Each flake a page, a tale unfolds,
In silhouettes where silence holds.

The moonlight casts a spell of grace,
Filling the world, a bright embrace,
While shadows dance on glimmered snow,
These fables whisper what we know.

With every breath, a word takes flight,
In frosty air, in the still night,
The gentle breeze carries the lore,
Of loves once lost, and dreams in store.

Among the trees, a secret kept,
In snowy blankets softly wept,
Alabaster truths await the dawn,
To find the light, where hope is drawn.

These fables weave through time and space,
With every heart, a softer place,
In winter's grasp, the stories twine,
In shining light, they choose to shine.

Luminous Traces on Coated Glass

In morning light, the edges gleam,
Reflections dance like fleeting dreams.
A world outside, yet here I stay,
Within these frames, the shadows play.

Waves of color, softly spread,
On every pane, the past is led.
Ghosts of moments, bright and faint,
On coated glass, where visions paint.

The sunbeams trace a tender path,
Warmth erupts in the aftermath.
Each glimmer holds a silent tale,
Of wishes born, and hopes that sail.

Underneath, the world looks clear,
Yet hidden truths are very near.
Through layers thick, the light finds ways,
To carve a journey in the haze.

With every breath, the glass reveals,
A story told in quiet meals.
Fragments linger, memories cling,
In luminous traces, life will sing.

Awakened Fortunes in the Cold

Frosted nights greet weary souls,
Whispers weave through icy poles.
Yet in the chill, a spark ignites,
Awakening warmth in frozen sights.

Under blankets, dreams take flight,
Through stillness, fears lose their bite.
Each breath a cloud, each sigh a song,
A fortune found where hearts belong.

Crystalline stars shimmer bright,
Guiding the lost into the light.
Every step on a path so bold,
Leads to riches, treasures untold.

From barren trees, the promise grows,
In silent whispers, nature flows.
Through winter's grip, hope will unfold,
Awakened fortunes in the cold.

In solitude, the spirit thrives,
Life's hidden treasures rekindle lives.
As the sun starts to break the mold,
New tales emerge, as dreams are sold.

Rhythms of Whispered White

Softly falling, the snowflakes play,
With graceful dances, they drift away.
Silence echoes in every flake,
In nature's hush, new paths we make.

Whispering winds caress the night,
Blanketing earth in purest white.
Underneath stars, the world finds peace,
In rhythmic breaths, all troubles cease.

Each flurry holds a secret tune,
Sung by the hearth, or under moon.
Journeying forth on a canvas bright,
Carving dreams in the still of night.

Frozen moments, gently spun,
In the embrace of the winter sun.
The heartbeats thrumming, standing still,
With every whisper, we bend to will.

In quiet intervals, life aligns,
Nature's pulse in myriad signs.
With rhythms soft, in white's embrace,
We find our solace, our sacred space.

Silent Stories in the Glaze

In every crack, a tale resides,
Underneath layers where laughter hides.
Muffled echoes play their part,
In silent stories, we keep close to heart.

The glaze reflects our woven lives,
Capturing secrets, where time thrives.
Each bubble forms a fleeting laugh,
Frozen moments, a cherished draft.

Artistry born of craftsmanship,
Tales of joy, and hardship's grip.
In every hue, a memory stays,
Behind the shine, life's tender rays.

Veiled histories wait to be told,
In porcelain warmth, in shadows bold.
As we touch the surface, we feel,
The silent stories, now revealed.

A tapestry spun in vibrant glaze,
Holds fragments of our yesterdays.
In every piece, we find our place,
With silent wonders, time we embrace.

Secrets Encased in Ice

In a world where whispers hide,
Frozen tales the winds confide,
Buried deep beneath the snow,
Silent secrets yearn to flow.

Glistening shards of light and sheen,
Reveal what once had never been,
Each fracture tells the tale of old,
In icy silence, stories unfold.

Beneath the frost, emotions lie,
In stillness where the echoes cry,
Captured moments trapped in time,
Each breath a gesture, cold yet prime.

A crystal cage around life's breath,
Holds joys and sorrows, love and death,
Unraveled truths, they twist and spin,
In shivers vast, the heart begins.

So walk with care on this thin ice,
For hidden dreams, they're worth the price,
The warmth of thought ignites the chill,
And secrets dance with winter's will.

Ghosts of the Frosted Pines

In shadows where the moonlight bends,
The pines stand tall, they are old friends,
Whispers haunt the frosted air,
Echoes dance with nature's flair.

With every gust, a sigh is heard,
Stray echoes of a mighty bird,
Among the branches, they retreat,
To secrets lost, where memories meet.

Beneath the cloak of winter's chill,
Ghosts linger near, a silent thrill,
Telling tales of winter's nights,
And woven dreams in silver lights.

Their laughter hides in softest snow,
As shadows flit where breath refuses flow,
In stillness deep, their stories glide,
Through frosted pines, where dreams reside.

So tread with care on this old ground,
For here the lost are always found,
Their spectral forms, a friendly plea,
In winter's grasp, they wander free.

The Quiet Echo of Crystal Dawn

Amidst the frost, a silence stirs,
As dawn awakens, the world blurs,
Each ray of light, a soft embrace,
In crystal dawn's lingering grace.

The earth adorned in shimmering white,
Awakens dreams to greet the light,
With every breath, the day ignites,
In tranquil tones and gentle sights.

A whisper shared on morning air,
Invites the heart, it calls us there,
To listen close, and feel the beat,
As echoes rise beneath our feet.

The world unfolds with fragile care,
In winter's arms, we pause and stare,
For every dew that glimmers bright,
Holds echoes of the moonlit night.

In quietude, the spirit soars,
Through crystal dawn, we find what's yours,
Awake in beauty's softening glow,
In tranquil moments, life will flow.

Winter's Veil Over Silent Waters

A shroud of white, a gentle quilt,
Covers the ground where dreams are built,
Silent waters, still and deep,
Hold the secrets that winter keeps.

Glistening edges of the lake,
Reflecting skies, still as they wake,
Each ripple tells a tale anew,
In winter's clutch, so calm and true.

The wind hushed down beneath its weight,
While icy fingers slowly sate,
The thirst for peace, an untold wish,
Where shadows rest and moments finish.

Birds nestle close in frosted trees,
While nature hums a melody,
Wrapped in stillness, the world holds tight,
To whispers soft as stars ignite.

So gaze upon these silent streams,
Where winter weaves the fabric of dreams,
In every glance, a story spun,
As winter veils the setting sun.

Shivering Truths Cast in Ice

In winter's breath, the truth unfolds,
Beneath the frost, a story holds.
Silent echoes, lost in time,
Whispers caught in crystal rhyme.

Frigid nights, the shadows creep,
Secrets buried, dark and deep.
Glacial forms, they shatter light,
Revealing paths through endless night.

In icy shards, the past is clear,
Frozen tales, we hold so dear.
Shivering truths, a chilling grace,
In every flake, a hidden face.

Time stands still in this cold embrace,
Each breath a fog, a haunting space.
From frozen depths, we start to see,
The echoes of what used to be.

With every breeze, the silence knows,
A story wrapped in winter's clothes.
In shivering truths, we find our way,
Through icy realms where shadows play.

Constellations in a Chilled Dreamscape

In twilight's glow, the stars appear,
A canvas painted, cold yet clear.
Dreamscape whispers, night's allure,
Constellations bright, they call us pure.

Drifting through the frozen skies,
Celestial dances, ancient ties.
In every twinkle, solace found,
A cosmic lullaby, profound.

Beneath the veil of silver frost,
We search for moments not yet lost.
In starlit paths, we wander far,
Guided by night's eternal star.

The chill embraces, dreams take flight,
In endless realms of pure starlight.
Each constellation tells a tale,
In whispered winds, we set our sail.

Through frosted air, our spirits soar,
In dreamscapes vast, we yearn for more.
Connect the dots, the universe,
In this frozen night, a sacred verse.

Frosted Whispers of the Ancients

In the stillness of the dawn,
Frosted whispers linger on.
Echoes from the days of yore,
Ancient tales forevermore.

Through misty woods and silent glades,
In every tundra, history fades.
Footprints lost beneath the chill,
Yet, in the silence, voices thrill.

Snowflakes dance on whispers sweet,
Carrying secrets, bittersweet.
From the frost, old stories rise,
As time unravels, wisdom flies.

On frosty winds, the ancients call,
Their echoes wrap around us all.
Each breath we take, a bond we share,
In winter's grip, we learn to care.

Through frosted air, we seek the past,
Embracing stories, shadows cast.
In every whisper, we find our way,
Through ancient realms, where memories play.

Whispers of a Frozen Heart

In the depths where silence grows,
Lies a heart that seldom shows.
Frozen veins and icy trails,
Amidst the whispers, love unveils.

Shattered dreams in frostbite held,
Emotions masked, yet still compelled.
Every heartbeat, a silent plea,
In winter's grasp, longing to be free.

Through winter nights, the shadows creep,
Awakening fears that make us weep.
Yet in the cold, a light can spark,
A glimmer found within the dark.

Echoes of warmth, once held near,
Trace the contours of every tear.
In frozen silence, hopes ignite,
Whispers soft as stars unite.

The thaw will come, the ice will break,
In the hush, a chance to wake.
With each whisper, the heart will mend,
In frozen realms, love has no end.

Translucent Dreams Defying Time

In the haze of dawn's embrace,
Whispers dance in crystal light.
Shadows stretch beyond their place,
Reality shimmers, taking flight.

Moments weave like threads of silk,
Memory pools in twilight's glow.
Hearts entwined, soft as milk,
Through the ages, we shall flow.

Ghostly echoes, fleeting sighs,
Chasing shadows, lost in bliss.
In the silence, laughter flies,
Each dream born from a tender kiss.

Stars align in fragile grace,
Time transcends its heavy chains.
We merge in a warm embrace,
Defying what remains.

Wanderers in glowing hues,
Treading paths of velvet night.
We craft our fate, we shape our views,
In translucent dreams, we find our light.

The Quiet Echo of Icy Dusk

Beneath the weight of silver skies,
A hush blankets the evening glow.
Moonlit whispers, soft goodbyes,
Dancing where the cold winds blow.

Frosted leaves in silence twirl,
Crystals spark in gentle dusk.
Nature's breath—both soft and whirl,
In the chill, a tranquil husk.

Stars emerge, so bold, so bright,
Filling voids with tender gleams.
Every shimmer holds a light,
Illuminating hidden dreams.

Through the quiet, hearts align,
Time slows down, a sacred pause.
In the stillness, love will shine,
Echoing without a cause.

Embrace the chill, let it seep,
Into cracks of human souls.
In icy dusk, our secrets keep,
As the night quietly unfolds.

Infinitesimal Reflections of Cold

In the mirror of frozen streams,
Time lingers like a sweet refrain.
Each ripple holds a thousand dreams,
Reflections whispering in the rain.

Petals pressed in icy breath,
Nature's artifacts of grace.
In the silence of untimely death,
Life's essence finds its place.

Glistening shards of brittle glass,
Capture moments, fleeting, small.
Every glimmer, every pass,
Transitory, yet so enthralled.

Winds of winter softly speak,
Carrying tales through the night.
In the stillness, hearts grow weak,
Yearning for warmth, seeking light.

Infinitesimal fragments gleam,
Underneath the moon's embrace.
In each drop, a world may seem,
The cold a gentle, tender lace.

Colorless Emotions in Winter's Breath

Fog rolls in with a muted grace,
Wrapping thoughts in veils of white.
Frozen shadows find their place,
Drifting in the quiet night.

Words float like snowflakes down,
Landing soft on empty ground.
In the silence, a worn frown,
Echoes of the lost profound.

Each heartbeat, a colorless hue,
Painting dreams in shades of gray.
In the frost, emotions brew,
Hidden drops of yesterday.

Hope flickers, a candle's ghost,
Through the winter's bitter chill.
In the silence, we crave the most,
Moments when time stands still.

Colorless, our spirits sigh,
But within each breath, a spark.
In winter's grasp, we learn to fly,
Finding warmth within the dark.

Solitude Beneath the Skies

In the quiet night, stars gleam bright,
Whispers of the wind sing soft lullabies.
Alone with my thoughts, just me and the night,
The peace of the dark, where my spirit flies.

Moon beams like silver, trace shadows that play,
Each glimmer a promise of dreams yet to find.
In solitude's arms, I quietly sway,
Carried away by the stillness, unconfined.

Clouds drift above, a gentle parade,
Painting the canvas of an endless plane.
Here in the calm, my worries all fade,
Lost in the vastness, free from the chain.

The world feels so distant, a fading refrain,
With every deep breath, I let go and soar.
In solitude's realm, I'm learning again,
To cherish the silence, to seek out the core.

Beneath the wide skies, a heart finds its voice,
In the echo of night, where the secrets unfold.
A dance in the quiet, a moment of choice,
To live in the now, to be brave and bold.

Frigid Memories in Still Waters

In the frozen depths, reflections lie,
Echoes of laughter, now distant and cold.
Ripples of time that the seasons defy,
Frigid the memories that once were so bold.

Silent the water, a blanket of ice,
Shimmering softly with whispers of yore.
Each glint tells a tale, a fragment of spice,
Of moments long past, lost on the shore.

Beneath the still surface, stories entrap,
Faces of lovers, of joys and of fears.
Trapped in this silence, as time takes its nap,
Frigid the feelings, yet warm are the tears.

Nature conceals what the heart wishes loud,
Beneath the thick layer, emotions run deep.
In still waters' cradle, I'm wrapped like a shroud,
Awake in the night, where my memories sleep.

Frozen the moments, yet vivid the pain,
In the heart of the winter, where echoes abide.
A symphony played on the icy terrain,
Frigid and tender, my memories glide.

Dreams Encased in Ice

In the grip of winter, dreams start to form,
Encased in the crystal, untouched by the sun.
Each desire a flicker, waiting for warmth,
Hopes held together, yet feeling so spun.

Frozen ambitions, like stars in the night,
In the stillness they linger, so delicate, frail.
Wrapped in the frost, hidden out of sight,
Yearning for freedom, too timid to sail.

Time drips like icicles, hanging so clear,
Moments suspended, a silent ballet.
Inside this cocoon, I wrestle with fear,
Dreams encased in ice, just waiting for May.

Whispers of spring tease the cold of my heart,
Longing to break free, to melt into light.
Each day a reminder, we're never apart,
Dreams encased in ice, ready for flight.

As the seasons turn, I'll cast off this shell,
Let warmth touch my spirit, renew what I chase.
From dreams I've held dear, I'll bid them farewell,
Embrace the soft spring, a vibrant embrace.

Transparent Lives Behind Frost

Behind the glass window, a world we can't see,
Lives intertwined in a frosty embrace.
Each breath creates whispers, a muted decree,
Stories unfolding in this serene place.

Icicles hanging like curtains of light,
Shielding the warmth from the world outside.
Behind them are souls, in their private flight,
Transparent their lives, where no one can hide.

Through the fogged-up panes, the shadows do sway,
Silent the laughter, the joy and the pain.
Each moment a layer, that time can't allay,
Lives in a bubble, from sunshine to rain.

Glimmers of hope peek through chilly designs,
Promises stitched into the fabric of frost.
In the heart of the cold, a flicker that shines,
Transparent lives, seeking warmth, never lost.

So let the cold settle, let the frost be our friend,
Each crystalline wonder a glimpse of our core.
In the hush of the winter, our stories transcend,
Transparent lives thriving, forever, explore.

Wind-Kissed Dreams on Frozen Faces

Whispers of chill dance through the air,
While snowflakes twirl, a graceful affair.
Hopes like feathers drift and glide,
In the winter's heart, where dreams abide.

Faces aglow with a frosty sheen,
Painted in hues of silver and green.
The world around, a canvas of white,
Where wishes bloom in the pale moonlight.

Rustle of branches, a soft, sweet song,
Carried by breezes, mysterious and strong.
Echoes of laughter ring through the trees,
As children play in the heart of the freeze.

Memories whisper in the quiet night,
Softly illuminated by starlit light.
Each breath a promise of warmth soon to come,
As time dances on to a wintery drum.

Embrace the chill with a smile so bright,
For morning will break with a golden light.
Wind-kissed dreams on faces aglow,
In the silent embrace of falling snow.

Beneath the Ice, a Heart Beats On

Under thick layers of ice and snow,
Lies the pulse of life, steady and slow.
Nature's secret, a heartbeat's song,
Beneath the surface, where it belongs.

Even in cold, warmth still resides,
In frozen chambers where love abides.
Beneath the frost, the essence of spring,
Awaits the moment when life will take wing.

Silent are the whispers of time,
Yet in the depths, there's rhythm and rhyme.
Roots that dig deep through the slumbering earth,
Shall rise once more to embrace rebirth.

The ice may sparkle, a beautiful guise,
But beneath it all, a soul never dies.
The heart beats on beneath the snow's quilt,
A testament to all the love built.

So wait in patience, for warmth will appear,
The thaw of the seasons, drawing near.
In the quiet depth where true life belongs,
Beneath the ice, the heart sings its songs.

Haunting Echoes of a Snow-Muffled World

In the stillness where shadows creep,
Snow blankets the earth in a slumber deep.
Every footfall fades to a whisper,
As the world breathes softly, a chillier sister.

Haunting echoes ring through the trees,
A symphony composed by the winter breeze.
The air is thick with stories untold,
Of the glories and sorrows that winter holds.

Silence embraces each minute and hour,
While frost weaves wonders, a crystalline flower.
The landscape holds secrets, both ancient and new,
In the hush of the snow, all becomes true.

Ghostly figures dance in the pale moonlight,
In the realm of dreams, where day meets night.
Each breath a cloud in the world of the still,
Carrying whispers of warmth and chill.

The beauty lies deep within every flake,
A reminder that life must sometimes break.
In this snow-muffled world, let us be bold,
And embrace haunting tales, both fragile and old.

Glinting Shadows in the Winter Sun

Caught in the glow of a low winter sun,
Shadows stretch long, as day has begun.
Glinting like diamonds on snow-covered ground,
A world of enchantment, vivid and profound.

Footprints imprint where the warmth finds a way,
Marking the path of a bright new day.
In the twinkle of light, stories unfold,
Of icy adventures and treasures untold.

Branches are laden with glittering frost,
While time slips gently, never lost.
The beauty of winter, a fleeting scene,
Captured in moments, serene and keen.

Children burst forth with laughter and glee,
Creating their castles of white jubilee.
Every glance reveals nature's playful art,
As glinting shadows awaken the heart.

The winter sun dips, casting colors so bright,
Painting the skies with radiant light.
In the fading glow, warmth lingers on,
In glinting shadows, our spirits are drawn.

Crystal Visions in Stillness

In the dawn's soft embrace, glowing light,
Whispers of dreams in the crystal bright.
Reflections shimmer in silent streams,
Caught in a moment, stitched into dreams.

Glistening patterns on icy glass,
Echoes of time that gently pass.
Each sigh of the wind, a tale foretold,
In the stillness, secrets unfold.

Luminous shards dance in the air,
Fleeting glimpses of wonder, rare.
Casting a spell, the world feels new,
In crystal visions, reality's hue.

Amidst the quiet, a heartbeat's sound,
Vibrations of hopes in stillness found.
Life's gentle pulse beneath the frost,
In those moments, we find what is lost.

When twilight descends, shadows play,
Carving the silence as night claims the day.
In crystal colors, the universe spins,
In the stillness, the magic begins.

Hues of the Chilling Horizon

Violet whispers, dawn's first breath,
Painting the sky, a dance with death.
Hues of longing in the cool air,
Brushstrokes of nature, a tender flair.

Orange blush upon edges of night,
Stretching the shadows in muted light.
The horizon sings of stories untold,
In chilling embraces, both fierce and bold.

Emerald dreams where the chill meets the sea,
A canvas of calm, setting our hearts free.
Each wave that crashes, a sigh from the deep,
Hues of the horizon, secrets we keep.

In twilight's grip, the colors unite,
Creating a symphony, dark to bright.
A spectrum of feelings, the pulse of the sky,
Hues of the chilling horizon, we fly.

Witness the magic, let your soul soar,
Feel the chill whisper; crave for more.
In the painting of life, exquisite and wide,
Hues of the horizon, forever our guide.

Glistening Shadows of the Past

Beneath the surface, memories glow,
Echoes of laughter from long ago.
In shadows that linger, they softly kiss,
Glistening tales of a time we miss.

Wrapped in whispers, stories unfold,
Fragments of life, both gentle and bold.
Flickering moments, a dance with the dusk,
Glistening shadows, nostalgia's trust.

Through golden leaves where memories sway,
A tapestry woven from yesterday.
Each shimmering thread, a heart's deepest wish,
In glistening shadows, linger and swish.

Twilight descends with a comforting hand,
Guiding our thoughts to a promised land.
In the hush of the evening, we hear the call,
Glistening shadows echo, embracing us all.

In those dark corners, the glimmers stay,
Guiding our spirits, lighting the way.
Through glistening shadows, we learn to rise,
And weave our futures beneath the skies.

Submerged Whispers in Chill

Under the surface, secrets reside,
Whispers of water where dreams often hide.
Echoes of silence in the deep blue,
Submerged thoughts that drift, lost from view.

Crystals of ice that shimmer so bright,
Holding the warmth of the fading light.
In chill's embrace, the heartbeats slow,
Submerged whispers, a haunting glow.

Beneath the waves where the world feels still,
The currents guide every hidden thrill.
A dance with shadows in the icy swell,
Submerged whispers weave their own spell.

In the depths where the forgotten wait,
Each ripple carries a weighty fate.
With the chill of the depths, a soft kiss,
Submerged whispers, an ocean of bliss.

Gather the echoes, let them unfold,
A story of peace in waters cold.
Submerged in whispers, our souls align,
In the chill of the depths, we gently shine.

Glacial Echoes in the Cavern of Time

In shadows deep where silence reigns,
  Whispers of frost call out my name.
 A cavern vast, where echoes dwell,
  Time stands still, a frozen spell.

The ice reflects each fleeting thought,
  Captured moments, dearly sought.
   Nature's breath, a secret song,
  In glacial halls, we all belong.

Each crystal shard, a story told,
Of ancient trees and glaciers bold.
In this embrace of cold and light,
I find my peace, my soul's delight.

Beneath the weight of fractured sky,
  The past resounds; it drifted by.
 Yet in this stillness, hope persists,
 A dance of time that still exists.

In icy chambers, dreams reside,
And there I walk, with time as guide.
Glacial echoes, I hear them clear,
  In harmony, I have no fear.

Nature's Chill, a Reflected Calm

The world is wrapped in winter's shawl,
Each breath a mist, a silvery thrall.
Beneath the weight of cold's embrace,
Nature whispers, slows the pace.

The branches bend with frosted tips,
Silent echoes on frosty lips.
A tranquil world, it softly sighs,
Underneath the slate-gray skies.

In the hush, the stillness grows,
As quiet as the falling snows.
Time slips gently, unaware,
In nature's chill, we find our care.

Reflections dance on icy streams,
Where sunlight weaves through waking dreams.
Each glimmer speaks of things unseen,
A calm that flows, eternally green.

Here in the frost, the heart takes flight,
Cradled close by the frost's soft light.
Nature holds, in arms so wide,
A peace within the winter's pride.

The Calm Beneath the Ice

Beneath the surface, stillness reigns,
A world of quiet, free from chains.
In icy depths, the secrets lie,
Where life persists, though the cold winds sigh.

Translucent layers, a frozen cloak,
Silent tales in whispers spoke.
The water breathes, a hidden grace,
In the heart of winter's embrace.

The ice, a mirror of what may be,
Reflecting dreams, both wild and free.
As nature rests, the thoughts take flight,
In this calm, we find our light.

A gentle hum beneath the cold,
A vibration of stories old.
In tranquil depths, our spirits soar,
Through icy barriers, we explore.

Here lies the peace, profound and true,
The calm beneath, an endless view.
In frozen stillness, we arise,
To seek the warmth of hidden skies.

Snowflakes Dancing through Memory

Snowflakes swirl in the crisp night air,
Each one unique, a moment rare.
They whisper soft of days gone by,
As winter's breath begins to sigh.

They twirl like dreams upon the breeze,
Painting memories with gentle ease.
Drifting down, they softly kiss,
The world transformed in serene bliss.

A tapestry of white unfolds,
Each flake a story, untold gold.
They dance and play, in moonlit scenes,
Reviving joy in our forgotten dreams.

With every flake, a chance to feel,
The warmth of life, the snow's ideal.
In winter's grip, we find our way,
As snowflakes guide us through the gray.

Their delicate forms grace the earth,
A reminder of love, life, and mirth.
In this dance of time, we find our way,
Through snowflakes soft, we shall not stray.

The Silent Dance of the Northern Winds

Whispers float on the frosty air,
A gentle hush fills the night rare.
The stars above twinkle in delight,
As shadows sway in the pale moonlight.

Silent breezes brush through the trees,
Carrying secrets from far-off seas.
They swirl and glide, a mystical flight,
Painting the world in silver and white.

In the stillness, a melody plays,
Echoing softly through ancient ways.
Each gust a note, each hush a refrain,
A tranquil song in the vast, cold plain.

Frozen dreams in a blanket of dark,
Every flicker a whisper, a spark.
The northern winds weave tales untold,
In the embrace of the night so cold.

With every breath, the night holds tight,
The silent dance, a wondrous sight.
Nature's symphony in perfect blend,
Where time stands still, and spirits mend.

Celestial Ice Patterns Above

In the stillness, ice glimmers bright,
Crafted by stars in the cloak of night.
Patterns fragile, yet boldly they show,
An ethereal art, forever aglow.

Celestial dreams in a frozen gaze,
Dancing lights in a shimmering haze.
Each spire and flake a story, a song,
In the twilight where shadows belong.

Below the vast sky, the earth holds her breath,
While ice takes form, a promise of depth.
In shimmering blues, the heavens reflect,
A breathtaking view we cannot reject.

Ephemeral beauty, a fleeting glance,
Nature's canvas forever in dance.
A fleeting moment, but etched in our mind,
The icy patterns, both vivid and kind.

Above the world, where whispers reside,
Celestial wonders in beauty abide.
With hearts open wide, we gaze and admire,
As the night unfolds, setting dreams on fire.

A Tapestry of Stars on a Frozen Night

A tapestry woven of silver and gold,
Under the cloak of the night so bold.
Stars are the stitches in fabric divine,
In the chill of the air, their beauty shines.

Each constellation, a story retold,
Of heroes and legends, of dreams that unfold.
In the vastness, whispers of light,
Glimmers of hope in the deep, dark night.

Frigid winds carry tales of the past,
Under this night sky, forever vast.
We lie on the snow, wrapped in the glow,
As the universe dances, gentle and slow.

A moment suspended in time and space,
Lost in the wonder of nature's grace.
With every heartbeat, the cosmos aligns,
In the embrace of the stars, our fate intertwines.

Frozen breath mingles in the chill air,
As we weave our dreams without a care.
A tapestry bright on this night divine,
With hearts full of wonder, forever we shine.

Through the Crystal Dome of Time

Through the crystal dome where whispers dwell,
Time bends and dances, casting its spell.
Moments crystallize in soft, whispered sighs,
Reflecting the light of a thousand skies.

Frozen seconds slip softly away,
In the embrace of the night, they play.
Beneath the stars, where memories bloom,
Echoes of laughter fill every room.

Each heartbeat a note in the symphony grand,
As time intertwines, like grains of sand.
Through the dome of ice, our dreams take flight,
Illuminated by the softest light.

In the vast expanse of the still night air,
We find our solace, a moment rare.
Through these glimmering halls, we travel slow,
Reliving stories that gently flow.

Time whispers secrets that few can decode,
Within the shelter of the crystal road.
Together we wander through ages sublime,
In this frozen realm, beyond the reach of time.

Ephemeral Beauty in Frozen Frames

In the light of dawn's embrace,
Shadows dance with fleeting grace.
Colors blend, then fade away,
Moments live, then softly sway.

Capturing whispers in the air,
Memories caught, a breath to share.
Frozen smiles in a glassy tear,
Time's canvas we hold dear.

Each petal drapes in icy lace,
Nature's sigh, a soft redress.
In the stillness, beauty gleams,
Life unfolds in fragile dreams.

Glimmers shine on winter's breath,
An artful dance that hints of death.
Yet in the silence, sweet and bright,
Ephemeral beauty takes its flight.

In the heart's embrace we find,
Frames of grace our souls remind.
Cherished scenes that twist and bend,
Ephemeral beauty, never end.

Silent Crystals of the Soul

Within the heart, reflections gleam,
Silent whispers in a dream.
Crystals form in shadows deep,
Memories, a vigil keep.

Softly twinkling in the night,
Flickering stars, a guiding light.
Each facet holds a tale unwritten,
A silence where love's softly smitten.

Glistening tears of joy and pain,
Nature's chorus in the rain.
Fragments of what's long been lost,
Found in the frost, oh, what a cost.

In the stillness, echoes play,
Tender songs of yesterday.
Crystals speak where words can't go,
A secret that the heart will know.

Silent moments vibrate, swell,
Infinite stories needing to tell.
In the quiet, beauty calls,
Crystals shine as silence falls.

Dimmed Echoes of the North

Whispers carried on the breeze,
Bringing tales from distant trees.
Frosty winds that weave and sway,
Dimmed echoes of the past's ballet.

Northern lights, a ghostly glow,
Haunting dreams they softly sow.
With each pulse, a memory stirs,
In the silence, the soul concurs.

Cold as ice, yet warm inside,
Frozen dreams that won't subside.
Nature's breath, a lullaby,
Songs of old that never die.

Mountains rise with ancient pride,
Guarding secrets, hope's abide.
Echoes whisper, strong yet frail,
In their chant, we find the tale.

As the twilight softly creeps,
Listen close, the Northland sleeps.
In each shadow, nothing's lost,
In dimmed echoes, we pay the cost.

Frost's Tender Caress of the Mind

In the quiet of the night,
Frost whispers with tender light.
Gentle touch on weary brow,
Cleansing thoughts of here and now.

Snowflakes fall like softest sighs,
Painting words where silence lies.
In the chill, clarity grows,
Frost recalls what nature knows.

A delicate chill, a cool embrace,
Wrapping dreams in crystal lace.
Each thought a snowflake, pure and bright,
Frost's caress ignites the light.

Moments freeze, yet time is fleet,
In winter's hold, the heart's retreat.
Calming depths of frozen streams,
Frost unveils the hidden dreams.

In this stillness, peace aligns,
Encased in frost, the mind defines.
With each breath, the world unwinds,
Frost's tender caress, a gift of kinds.

The Quiet Breath of Winter's Embrace

Whispers of frost in the chilling air,
Softly they weave through the twilight glare.
Blankets of silence cover the ground,
In this hushed moment, peace can be found.

Bare branches shiver with frosty delight,
Twinkling stars beckon in the deep night.
A hush falls gently, the world holds its breath,
Cradled in beauty, enchantment in depth.

Snowflakes dance lightly, a delicate waltz,
Each one unique, without any faults.
The world is a canvas, serene and white,
In winter's embrace, everything feels right.

Footsteps are muffled on the soft, white sheet,
Echoes of wonder, in silence, they meet.
Time drifts like snowflakes, both fragile and free,
In winter's quiet heart, pure tranquility.

The breath of the season, slow and profound,
In the stillness of night, true magic is found.
Cocooned in the chill, I find my reprieve,
In the quiet of winter, I choose to believe.

Snowy Serenity in the Mirror of Stillness

Nature is wrapped in a blanket of light,
A tranquil hush falls, embracing the night.
Each flake a secret, a tale to unfold,
In the mirror of stillness, pure magic behold.

The moon casts a glow on the pristine white,
Illuminating dreams tucked away from sight.
Footprints of wanderers trail through the calm,
Each step echoes softly, a sweet, quiet balm.

Gentle the night, like a lullaby sung,
In the heart of the winter, life's songs become young.
Crystals like diamonds shimmer and gleam,
Reflecting our hopes, like a sweet, frozen dream.

Branches hang low, adorned with frost's lace,
Nature's quiet beauty, a wondrous embrace.
The whispering winds share stories anew,
In snowy serenity, the world feels so true.

In the quiet of winter, peace is bestowed,
As hearts find their rhythm on this gentle road.
Silence wrapped tightly in winter's white shroud,
In the mirror of stillness, we breathe softly, proud.

Ethereal Glimpses of Winter's Soul

Through the veil of frost, a shimmer appears,
Ethereal glimmers that silence our fears.
Winter whispers softly in colors so bold,
A symphony of beauty, a story retold.

In the dance of the snowflakes, magic unfolds,
Each flake a treasure, a secret that holds.
The breath of the cold, crisp and so bright,
Wraps around the heart like a warm, glowing light.

Mystic shadows stretch with the rise of the moon,
Echoes of winter in a soft, graceful tune.
Nature's design in shades of white and gray,
Ethereal glimpses that brighten the day.

In twilight's embrace, the world seems to pause,
Wrapped in the wonder, we ponder the cause.
What lies in the stillness of winter's sweet sighs?
Magic awaits in the depth of the skies.

Beneath the frost's blanket, life stirs with a dream,
Awakening softly, like a quiet stream.
In glimpses ethereal, wisdom is spun,
In winter's soft cradle, our hearts become one.

Mystic Reflections in a Frozen Realm

In a realm carved of ice, still waters reflect,
Whispers of frost, in a dance, they connect.
Each shimmer a story, a moment in time,
Mystic reflections in nature's sweet rhyme.

Crystalline surfaces beckon the gaze,
Embracing the night in a silvery haze.
Moonlight caresses the shadows that creep,
In this frozen sanctuary, the world falls asleep.

Glistening branches, a gallery of dreams,
Hope sparkles gently with silvered moonbeams.
The night's gentle charcoal is tender and deep,
In mystic reflections, our memories sweep.

The hush of the snow blankets echoes of sound,
Lay the heart open, to love that surrounds.
In the frozen embrace, find warmth in the cold,
In the mystery of winter, pure stories unfold.

As shadows grow longer, the day starts to wane,
Sparkling wonders remind us of change.
Mystic reflections in a frosted expanse,
In winter's quiet hold, we begin to dance.

Glacial Reverie

In whispers soft as frosted air,
A world of silence, pure and fair.
Ice crystals dance in winter's light,
Beneath the stars, the quiet night.

The moon reflects on icy streams,
Awakening the frost-kissed dreams.
A breath of chill, a fleeting thought,
Within this realm, our souls are caught.

Snowflakes twirl in elegant flight,
Natures brush in purest white.
Time freezes here, moments held fast,
A glacial reverie, unsurpassed.

The wind sings soft through barren trees,
Each note a ghost of summer's ease.
Yet in this cold, warmth can ignite,
Through tender hearts, we share the night.

With each dawn, the light will shift,
Bringing forth a gentle gift.
In this frozen world, we find
The beauty shared, our hearts entwined.

Shattered Ice Dreams

In twilight's glow, the shards do gleam,
Reflections of a frozen dream.
Each splinter tells a tale untold,
Of whispers lost in icy hold.

The glacier cracks, a thunderous sound,
Breaking silence in nature's ground.
Shards scatter, like hopes laid bare,
A moment's grace hangs in the air.

Beneath the surface, secrets sleep,
In frozen depths, their vigil keep.
Yet with each breath of warming sun,
The boundaries blur, the past is spun.

Fragile treasures, a world unspun,
Where dreams collide, and all are one.
Amidst the ice, a fire brews,
To melt the frost, to birth new views.

With every thaw, a chance to rise,
From shattered dreams beneath the skies.
Together we'll mend the fractured seams,
In the embrace of spring's sweet dreams.

Echoes Beneath the Frost

In silent woods where shadows creep,
Echoes of the past still sleep.
Beneath the frost, a story lies,
Whispers dance, as daylight dies.

The crackling ice, a fleeting sound,
Holds memories of worlds unbound.
Each footstep soft, the fallen snow,
A tale of yesterdays we know.

Branches bow with chilling weight,
Nature sighs in peaceful state.
Yet underneath, life bravely stirs,
Awaiting warmth, as spring-time purrs.

Frozen lakes, reflections caught,
In tranquil moments, solace sought.
We tread lightly on this path,
Where echoes linger, love's sweet wrath.

Hold tight the dreams that gently fade,
In frosty nights, memories made.
For when the thaw returns with grace,
The past will rise, take its place.

Mirrors of Winter's Grasp

In mirrors still, the world reflects,
A winter's tale, of cold effects.
The landscape carved in ice and snow,
A frozen canvas, time moves slow.

Each flake that falls, a story spun,
A fleeting glimpse of life begun.
The glittering sheen of winter's breath,
Under its charm lies silent death.

Branches crack and groan with weight,
Holding secrets of the late.
Yet in the stillness, new hope gleams,
A promise hidden within dreams.

The frost that kisses every bare,
Whispers softly of love and care.
Reflecting warmth in winter's chill,
A paradox, a heart to fill.

As morning breaks, the light will dance,
On mirrors created by chance.
In winter's grasp, we seek and find,
The beauty sharp, yet so aligned.